DUTCH OVEN COOKBOOK FOR BEGINNERS

40+ Simple, Quick, and Delicious Every Day One Pot Meal Recipes for Family's Health and Nourishment You Can Cook at Home, in Dutch Oven Cookbook Most Suitable for Beginners of All Ages.

Table of content

Introduction

You've bought the oven, washed, and seasoned it. What's next? What can I make? How do I go about making it?

Almost any dish can be cooked in a Dutch oven, from appetizers to desserts. You could use a set of different size Dutch ovens and racks to create an entire meal of 3 to 6 courses! Your favorites can be adapted to be cooked in an oven by varying the liquid content. An essential tip to keep in mind when cooking with a Dutch oven is to ensure that the stove is the correct size as per the recipe.

The Dutch oven is used to cook with or in –cooking with a Dutch oven entails placing the food directly into the oven while cooking in the range means that the food is placed into a second pan and then upon a trivet in the field.

The flavor and aroma of food cooked in a Dutch oven are second to none! But some rules need to be followed to ensure that the food cooked in a Dutch oven is lip-smacking good.

How to Use Dutch oven?

Let's begin with the meats prepared in a Dutch oven. Meat cooked in a Dutch oven has a unique taste and aroma; however, the cooking process within a Dutch oven is steaming when it must remember. The secret to making your meats look and taste great is to use flavorings and spices that complement the meat or poultry, but most importantly, ALWAYS BROWN THE MEAT FIRST!

How do I brown the meat in the oven? Easy, peasy –add bacon, oil, or any other preferred fat to the stove, ensuring that the furnace's bottom is covered. Heat the oven and then add the meat you want to cook and brown on all sides to seal in the juices. Once the meat has browned, drain any leftover fat dripping , season the meat with your chosen flavors and spices, place the lid on the oven and cook the meat. An approximate cooking time would be 30-35 minutes per pound of pork, beef, or lamb and 25-30 minutes per pound of poultry.

Now for your veggies. Vegetables can be steamed, boiled, or traditionally done in most Dutch ovens, and they are cooked in a sauce. You could also choose to bake or roast vegetables in the Dutch oven. The veggies cooked for approximately 3 minutes per inch of oven diameter; this means that a 20-inch stove filled with pumpkin cooked for 60 minutes, or a 15-inch oven filled with potatoes should cook for 45 minutes.

For vegetables cooked in sauce, e.g., sour cream potatoes or potatoes in a white sauce, the vegetables should be a boil. First, the water is discarded, and then the sauce is added to the veggies before they are cooked as per the usual method.

Mmmmm, the smell of freshly baked bread can get the appetite going! Bread, rolls, and biscuits made in a Dutch oven are perfect and have an old-world charm. The rule for bread making in a Dutch oven is "the larger the oven, the better for baking bread." The browning of bread in a Dutch oven requires altering the cooking process in the final minutes.

Recipes

Breakfast recipes

1. Saucy Pork Chops

(Hands-On Time: 10 mins| Cook Time: 5 mins | Servings 6)

Things We Need

- Five pork chops, deboned and trimmed 1 x 8 oz. can tomato sauce two green bell peppers, sliced one onion, sliced
- 3 tbsp. olive oil ¼ cup brown sugar
- 1 tbsp. apple cider vinegar 2 tsps. Worcestershire sauce 1½ tsps. salt
- 2 tbsps. cornstarch (optional)

How to Start

1. In a skillet, heat the olive oil over medium heat and brown the pork chops for about 5 minutes per side. Remove the chops to a Dutch oven and top with the green peppers and onion.

2. In a medium-sized bowl, mix the tomato sauce, vinegar, Worcestershire sauce, brown sugar, and salt. Pour the sauce over the chops and stir gently to coat the vegetables and meat.

3. Cook the chops on low for about 6 – 8 hours, then transfer to a serving dish and keep warm. Add the cornstarch to the gravy in the Dutch oven and whisk over low heat until the sauce thickens. Spoon the sauce over the vegetables and serve.

NUTRITIONAL VALUE PER SERVING

- CALORIES: 617
- PROTEIN: 10.9GRAMS
- FIBER: 12GRAMS
- NET CARBOHYDRATES:6.5GRAMS
- SUGAR ALCOHOL: 14.7GRAMS
- FAT: 55.8GRAMS
- SODIUM: 5 MG
- CARBOHYDRATES: 32.4GRAMS

- SUGAR: 2.7GRAMS

2. Potato Garlic puree

(Hands-On Time: 10 mins | Cook Time: 5 mins | Servings 6)

Things We Need

- 1 x 12 oz. can whole kernel corn two potatoes, diced
- One medium onion, diced
- 1¼ red chili peppers, minced two mugs vegetable broth
- 1 cup soy milk
- One clove garlic, minced 2½ tbsps margarine
- 2 tsps. parsley flakes
- 2 tsps. chili powder
- One ¼ tsps. salt

- Black pepper to taste
- Juice of 1 lime

How to Start

1. Place the vegetables, broth, salt, and spices into a Dutch oven, cover, and cook over low heat for 6 hours.
2. Pour the mixture into a blender, about ½ full, and blend to a puree. Puree the mixture in batches until smooth and return the pureed mixture to the Dutch oven, add in the soy milk and margarine and cook for an additional hour on low heat.
3. Add the lime juice just before serving.

NUTRITIONAL VALUE PER SERVING

- CALORIES: 617
- PROTEIN: 10.9GRAMS
- FIBER: 12GRAMS
- NET CARBOHYDRATES:6.5GRAMS
- SUGAR ALCOHOL: 14.7GRAMS
- FAT: 55.8GRAMS
- SODIUM: 5 MG
- CARBOHYDRATES: 32.4GRAMS
- SUGAR: 2.7GRAMS

3. Easy Peasy Bread

(Hands-On Time: 10 mins | Cook Time: 5 mins | Servings 6)

Things We Need

- Two mugs of all-purpose flour
- 1 cup warm water
- ¾ tsp. active dry yeast
- 1¼ tsps. salt
- ¾ tsp. chopped rosemary
- ¾ tsp. chopped sage
- ¾ tsp. chopped thyme

How to Start

1. Shift the dry Things We Need in a bowl. Add the herbs, if using, and water to make soft but pliable dough. The bowls cover with the help of a plastic wrap and set aside at room temperature overnight.

2. Transfer dough to a work surface generously sprinkled with flour. Fold the dough in half and struck and tuck to form a neat ball.

3. Sprinkle flour liberally over a kitchen towel and place dough onto the towel. Cover with a second well sprinkled kitchen towel and left aside to rise for about 2 hours; before baking, heat the oven at the temperature of 450°F. And place a covered Dutch oven into the oven to preheat. Remove from the oven once well heated, remove the lid and gently place the dough into the ungreased baking pan, seam side up. Shake the dish to ensure that the dough is evenly distributed.

4. Cover it and do bake for 30 minutes, then remove the lid and bake until a golden-brown crust forms. Remove from the baking dish and allow cooling before serving.

5. Makes one loaf

NUTRITIONAL VALUE PER SERVING

- CALORIES: 617
- PROTEIN: 10.9GRAMS
- FIBER: 12GRAMS
- NET CARBOHYDRATES:6.5GRAMS
- SUGAR ALCOHOL: 14.7GRAMS
- FAT: 55.8GRAMS
- SODIUM: 5 MG
- CARBOHYDRATES: 32.4GRAMS
- SUGAR: 2.7GRAMS

4. Saudi Chicken and Rice

(Hands-On Time: 10 mins| Cook Time: 5 mins | Servings 6)

Things We Need

- ½ tsp. ground cinnamon ½ tsp. ground allspice ½ tsp. saffron
- ¼ tsp. ground cardamom ½ tsp. ground white pepper ½ tsp. dried whole lime powder one whole chicken, cut into eight pieces ¼ cup butter
- ¼ cup tomato puree
- 14.5 oz. diced tomatoes, not drained six cloves garlic, minced
- One onion, finely chopped
- Three carrots, peeled and grated two whole cloves

- One pinch of ground nutmeg
- One pinch ground cumin
- One pinch ground coriander Salt & black pepper, to season 1 cube chicken bouillon
- Three ¼ mugs hot water
- Two ¼ mugs unrinsed Basmati rice
- ¼ cup raisins
- ¼ cup toasted, slivered almonds

How to Start

1. In a bowl, mix the cardamom, saffron, cinnamon, allspice, white pepper, and lime powder and set aside. Using a Dutch oven, melt the butter over medium heat, stir in the garlic and onion and cook until the onion has softened. Add in the chicken pieces and brown over medium-height heat for about 10 minutes.

2. Add the tomato puree and mix well. Add in the whole cloves, nutmeg, cumin, coriander, Kabsa spice mix, salt & black pepper, grated carrot, canned tomatoes with the juice, the chicken bouillon cube, and water. Bring the pot to a boil on less heat and leave to simmer, covered, for about 30 minutes. The chicken is done once the juices run clear. Gently add the rice in and stir

well. Cover and cook until the rice is tender and fluffy, and just about dry.

3. Add in the raisins and a little hot water, if required. Cover and simmer for a further 5-10 minutes or until the rice grains have separated. To serve, place the rice on a serving platter and arrange the chicken pieces on top. Garnish with the slivered almonds.

NUTRITIONAL VALUE PER SERVING

- CALORIES: 617
- PROTEIN: 10.9GRAMS
- FIBER: 12GRAMS
- NET CARBOHYDRATES:6.5GRAMS
- SUGAR ALCOHOL: 14.7GRAMS
- FAT: 55.8GRAMS
- SODIUM: 5 MG
- CARBOHYDRATES: 32.4GRAMS
- SUGAR: 2.7GRAMS

5. Worcestershire with Vegetables

(Hands-On Time: 10 mins | Cook Time: 5 mins | Servings 6)

Things We Need

- ½ cup all-purpose flour
- ½ cup vegetable oil Vegetables
- 1 cup chopped celery
- One green bell pepper, chopped
- 1 cup chopped green onions
- 1 tbsp. butter
- Tomato Sauce and Spices 1 x 8 oz. can tomato sauce 2 tbsp. Worcestershire sauce
- 1 tsp. Tabasco sauce two cloves garlic, minced 2 tsps. salt

- ½ tsp. dried thyme six mugs water Seafood and Okra
- 1 ½ lb. catfish, cut into 2-inch pieces
- 1 ½ lb. peeled and deveined shrimp
- 1 lb. chopped okra 1 tbsp. gumbo file powder
- ½ tsp. salt

How to Start

1. Add the vegetable oil into a Dutch oven, add in the flour.
2. Turn heat up to medium-high and place the oven on the burner. Cook, constantly stirring with a wooden spoon for about 10 minutes or until thick and bubbly and is dark brown.
3. Leave aside to cool and thicken. In a skillet over medium heat, melting the butter and add in the bell pepper, celery, and green onions and cook until tender. Add to the roux when done.
4. Add the tomato sauce, water, Worcestershire sauce, garlic, 2 tsps. salt, Tabasco sauce, and thyme to the vegetable mixture and bring to a gentle boil. To less the heat and allow to simmer for an hour.

5. Stir in the okra and cook for about 15 minutes, then add in the fish, stir gently, and cook till the flesh can be flaked with a fork.
6. Add in the shrimp and cook till they are bright pink—season with file powder and salt. Serve with boiled rice.

NUTRITIONAL VALUE PER SERVING
- CALORIES: 617
- PROTEIN: 10.9GRAMS
- FIBER: 12GRAMS
- NET CARBOHYDRATES:6.5GRAMS
- SUGAR ALCOHOL: 14.7GRAMS
- FAT: 55.8GRAMS
- SODIUM: 5 MG
- CARBOHYDRATES: 32.4GRAMS
- SUGAR: 2.7GRAMS

6. Beef Gumbo with cauliflower

(Hands-On Time: 10 mines| Cook Time: 5 mins | Servings 6)

Things We Need

- 4 lb. beef short ribs
- One head cauliflower chopped one onion, chopped
- Six cloves garlic, peeled
- Four green onions, chopped
- 1 cup basil leaves, chopped 2 tbsp. tomato paste 1 tsp. fish sauce
- 1 tsp. red curry paste two bay leaves
- 1-star anise
- 1 tsp. garam masala

- One pinch ground cayenne pepper Salt & black pepper to season
- 2 tsps. vegetable oil
- 1 cup coconut milk
- Two mugs of chicken broth

How to Start

1. Preheat the oven to 400° F and line a baking sheet with aluminum foil. Oil lightly.

2. The ribs are put on the baking sheet and season well with garam masala, salt, black pepper, and cayenne pepper. Bake in the preheated oven for 20 minutes or until well browned.

3. In a Dutch oven, combine the onion, tomato paste, red curry paste, and vegetable oil and cook over medium heat until the onion softens.

4. Add in the garlic cloves and cook till browned, then add in the bay leaves, star anise, broth, coconut milk, and fish sauce. Turn up the heat to medium-high and bring to a simmer. Add the ribs to the coconut milk mixture reduce the oven temperature to 300° F and bake till the ribs are tender, about 3 hours.

5. Remove from the oven and keep ribs to a bowl, and keep aside. Place the Dutch oven onto the stovetop over high heat. Skim any fat and remove any meat or bones left behind as it boils.

6. Add in the cauliflower, cover, and cook until the cauliflower is tender. Remove bones from the short rib and add the meat to the Dutch oven. Add in the green onions and basil leaves. Season with salt and pepper.

NUTRITIONAL VALUE PER SERVING

- CALORIES: 617
- PROTEIN: 10.9GRAMS
- FIBER: 12GRAMS
- NET CARBOHYDRATES:6.5GRAMS
- SUGAR ALCOHOL: 14.7GRAMS
- FAT: 55.8GRAMS
- SODIUM: 5 MG
- CARBOHYDRATES: 32.4GRAMS
- SUGAR: 2.7GRAMS

7. Cranberry Pot Roast

(Hands-On Time: 10 mins| Cook Time: 5 mins | Servings 6)

Things We Need

- 4 lb. beef chuck roast
- Three mugs beef broth
- 2 x 14.5 oz. can cranberry sauce
- 1 cup water
- One sweet onion, chopped
- 2 tbsp. vegetable oil
- 3 tbsp. all-purpose flour Salt & black pepper to taste

How to Start

1. In a Dutch oven, bring the beef broth and water to a boil over high heat. Add in the cranberry sauce and stir to dissolve. Cook over high heat.

2. Season the beef with salt and pepper and sprinkle the flour over evenly. In a skillet, heat the vegetable oil over medium heat and brown the roast on all sides. Transfer the roast into the Dutch oven with the chopped onion and cook until the meat comes away from the bones easily. The cooking time should be about 4 hours.

NUTRITIONAL VALUE PER SERVING

- CALORIES: 617
- PROTEIN: 10.9GRAMS
- FIBER: 12GRAMS
- NET CARBOHYDRATES:6.5GRAMS
- SUGAR ALCOHOL: 14.7GRAMS
- FAT: 55.8GRAMS
- SODIUM: 5 MG
- CARBOHYDRATES: 32.4GRAMS
- SUGAR: 2.7GRAMS

8. Chicken Dutch Roast

(Hands-On Time: 10 mins | Cook Time: 5 mins | Servings 6)

Things We Need

- 1 lb. chicken breast, skinless, boneless, cut into cubes two onions, chopped
- Two green bell peppers, chopped four carrots, julienned
- 1 cup brown sugar
- 1 cup orange juice
- 1 cup whiskey
- ¾ cup vinegar
- 1 tsp. red pepper flakes 2 tsps. ground ginger 1 tsp. toasted Asian sesame oil 2 ½ mugs water
- One ¼ mug white rice

- 1 tbsp. butter
- ½ cup orange juice
- 1 tbsp. cornstarch

How to Start

1. Use a Dutch oven and place the onions, bell peppers, and carrots into it.
2. Add in the chicken.
3. Whisk together 1 cup orange juice, brown sugar, vinegar, whiskey, ginger powder, red pepper flakes, and the sesame oil in a bowl. To transfer the mixture over the chicken and stir to mix the Things We Need—cover and place over medium-high heat to cook. Cook for about 90 minutes or until the chicken juices run clear.
4. Whilst the chicken is cooking, put the rice and water into a microwave-proof casserole dish and cook on high until the rice is tender and the water absorbed. Stir in the butter and toss.
5. the orange juice and cornstarch put in a bowl whisk together, add to the hot
6. Chicken mixture and cook until the sauce thickens. Serve the chicken over the hot buttered rice.

NUTRITIONAL VALUE PER SERVING

- CALORIES: 617
- PROTEIN: 10.9GRAMS
- FIBER: 12GRAMS
- NET CARBOHYDRATES:6.5GRAMS
- SUGAR ALCOHOL: 14.7GRAMS
- FAT: 55.8GRAMS
- SODIUM: 5 MG
- CARBOHYDRATES: 32.4GRAMS
- SUGAR: 2.7GRAMS

9. Bacon Flavored Chicken & Potatoes

(Hands-On Time: 10 mins | Cook Time: 5 mins | Servings 6)

Things We Need

- 12 slices center-cut bacon six chicken thighs
- Six chicken drumsticks one onion, coarsely chopped 1 ½ lb. baby Dutch yellow potatoes salt and black pepper to taste Seasoning Mix
- 2 tbsp. dried basil
- 2 tbsp. dried chives
- 1 tbsp. garlic powder
- 1 tbsp. Adobo seasoning
- 1 tbsp. ground black pepper

- 1 tsp. salt, to taste

How to Start

1. Preheat the oven to 400° F.

2. Wrap each piece of chicken in a slice of bacon, ensuring that the chicken is well covered with the bacon slices. Place the wrapped chicken pieces onto a baking pan to fit inside a Dutch oven— season with salt and pepper. Sprinkle the onion over the chicken pieces and push the potatoes into the spaces between the chicken pieces.

3. In a bowl, mix together the chives, garlic powder, basil, adobo seasoning, and black pepper and sprinkle over the chicken and potatoes. Place two bricks into the Dutch oven. Add in a cup of water and place the baking tray on the bricks. Cover and place into the preheated oven. Bake until the chicken is tender and the juices run clear. Remove the lid from the oven and allow the potatoes and bacon to be crisp and brown.

4. Serve hot.

NUTRITIONAL VALUE PER SERVING

- CALORIES: 617
- PROTEIN: 10.9GRAMS
- FIBER: 12GRAMS
- NET CARBOHYDRATES:6.5GRAMS
- SUGAR ALCOHOL: 14.7GRAMS
- FAT: 55.8GRAMS
- SODIUM: 5 MG
- CARBOHYDRATES: 32.4GRAMS
- SUGAR: 2.7GRAMS

10.　　Lamb Ragu

(Hands-On Time: 10 mins | Cook Time: 5 mins | Servings 6)

Things We Need

- 2 lb. stew lamb, cut into chunks 1x 28 oz. can be peeled whole plum tomatoes, two onions, chopped
- Eight cloves garlic
- One carrot
- 3 tbsp. sage four sprigs rosemary Olive oil
- Two mugs of red wine
- Salt and black pepper

How to Start

1. Coating the lamb chunks with salt and pepper and set them aside. Chop the onion and garlic coarsely and keep aside. Chop the carrot into thin rounds.

2. Using an ovenproof Dutch oven over medium heat, add enough olive oil to cover the bottom of the oven thinly. Add in the lamb once the oil is hot and brown well. Add in the onions and lower the heat to medium.

3. Allow cooking until the onions are golden; add in the rosemary and sage, garlic, and carrots. Reduce the heat further to medium-low and saut the vegetables until they are tender.

4. Add in the wine and simmer until the mixture is reduced by half. Use the spoon back or a fork to crush the tomatoes in the can, and then add the juices to the oven. After the cover, bring to a simmer, and place into a preheated oven, 275°F, for 3-4 hours.

5. Alternatively, leave to cook on the stovetop on high for about 4 hours or 8 hours on low.

6. Just before serving, use two forks to shred the chunks of meat, taste, and season if necessary.

7. Serve over pasta with ly grated Parmesan cheese.

NUTRITIONAL VALUE PER SERVING

- CALORIES: 617
- PROTEIN: 10.9GRAMS
- FIBER: 12GRAMS
- NET CARBOHYDRATES:6.5GRAMS
- SUGAR ALCOHOL: 14.7GRAMS
- FAT: 55.8GRAMS
- SODIUM: 5 MG
- CARBOHYDRATES: 32.4GRAMS
- SUGAR: 2.7GRAMS

11.   Mushroom Risotto

(Hands-On Time: 10 mins | Cook Time: 5 mins | Servings 6)

Things We Need

- ½ oz. Dried Porcini or Shiitake mushrooms, finely chopped ½ lb. Cremini mushrooms, cleaned and sliced 1 cup Arborio or a short-grain white rice four yellow onions
- Four cloves garlic, finely minced one sprig rosemary 1/3 cup olive oil
- ½ cup dry white wine
- 2 tbsp. balsamic vinegar two mugs vegetable broth
- Salt and black pepper to taste

How to Start

1. Preheat the oven to 300°F.

2. Rinse the dried mushrooms to remove any dust and place them into a bowl. Keep boiling water over and set aside to steep.

3. Finely dice one onion—heat 2 tbsp. olive oil in a 3-quart Dutch oven over medium heat. Add the onion and garlic to the oven and cook, stirring, for about 8-10 minutes or until the onions become translucent. Move to the side of the oven. The heats turn up to medium-high and add the sliced mushrooms to the oven and cook for 5 minutes without stirring. Give a quick stir and allow cooking for a further 5 minutes. They should be brown.

4. Drain the dried mushrooms but reserve the liquid. Add to the oven with a sprig of rosemary and saut   for a minute or two, mixing well. Add in the rice and cook for about 5 minutes, stirring occasionally. Turn the heat up to high and add in the broth, vinegar, white wine, and reserved water from the mushrooms. Stir and scrape the pan well to allow the "mushroomy" bits to be incorporated into the liquid. Season to taste. After

covering boil it and place into the preheated oven to bake for 35 minutes. Slice the remaining onions into half-moons. Heat the remaining olive oil in a cast-iron skillet and when hot, add in the onions and sprinkle well with salt. Lower the heat and allow to cook, occasionally stirring, until the onions turn a dark mahogany brown, about 30 minutes. Remove the risotto from the oven and let stand for 5 minutes, uncovered. Serve in bowls,

5. Garnish with the caramelized onions and a scoop of sour cream or whipped mascarpone and a dash of ground black pepper.

NUTRITIONAL VALUE PER SERVING

- CALORIES: 617
- PROTEIN: 10.9GRAMS
- FIBER: 12GRAMS
- NET CARBOHYDRATES:6.5GRAMS
- SUGAR ALCOHOL: 14.7GRAMS
- FAT: 55.8GRAMS
- SODIUM: 5 MG
- CARBOHYDRATES: 32.4GRAMS
- SUGAR: 2.7GRAMS

12. Chicken in Coconut Milk

(Hands-On Time: 10 mins| Cook Time: 5 mins | Servings 6)

Things We Need

- 3 lb. whole chicken
- Two green onions, chopped into ¼ inch pieces 6-8 cloves garlic, peeled and mashed
- One lemon, cut into eighths three mugs spinach leaves
- One bunch cilantro
- 5-inch lemongrass, white parts cut into ¼ inch pieces 16 oz. can coconut milk
- 4 tbsps. butter
- 1 tbsp. sesame or olive oil one cinnamon stick

- 2-star anise
- Sea salt and black pepper

How to Start

1. Clean, rinse and dry the chicken well. Sprinkle liberally with salt and pepper and place in the refrigerator overnight.

2. Preheat the oven to 375° F.

3. In a Dutch oven, melt the butter over medium heat; add in the oil, and then the chicken breast side up. Each side, Cook for about 30 seconds on each side, and remove from the oven and remove all the fat from the pan.

4. Place the chicken back into the oven with the star anise, cinnamon, and a handful of cilantro stems, lemon, garlic, lemongrass, and coconut milk. Cook in the preheated for 60-90 minutes. Baste the chicken every 20 minutes.

5. Ag the juices run clear, remove the chicken and place on a serving plate.

6. Remove the cinnamon stick and any other solids you prefer not to have.

7. Put the sauce back onto the stovetop, add in the spinach and allow it to wilt over medium heat.

8. Carve the chicken and serve with rice with the sauce spooned over the top.

9. Garnish with cilantro leaves.

NUTRITIONAL VALUE PER SERVING

- CALORIES: 617
- PROTEIN: 10.9GRAMS
- FIBER: 12GRAMS
- NET CARBOHYDRATES:6.5GRAMS
- SUGAR ALCOHOL: 14.7GRAMS
- FAT: 55.8GRAMS
- SODIUM: 5 MG
- CARBOHYDRATES: 32.4GRAMS
- SUGAR: 2.7GRAMS

13. Lamb, Bean & Bulgur Stew

(Hands-On Time: 10 mins| Cook Time: 5 mins | Servings 6)

Things We Need

- ½ lb. ground lamb 2/3 cup bulgur
- One medium onion, finely chopped
- 28 oz. Can diced plum tomatoes
- 14.5 oz. Can Gigante or Cannellini beans, drained and rinsed
- 5 oz. baby spinach
- 3½ oz. feta cheese, plus more for garnish
- 2 tbsps. extra-virgin olive oil
- 2 tsps. sweet paprika ¾ tsp. red-pepper flakes

- 1 tbsp. oregano leaves, plus more for garnish two mugs water
- Coarse salt and black pepper

How to start

1. In a Dutch oven, put oil to heat over medium heat. Add in the onions, lamb, bulgur, red-pepper flakes, and 1½ tsps. Salt and ½ tsp. pepper. Cook for 5 minutes, and stirring to break up the lamb.

2. Add paprika and stir until fragrant and roasted. Add in the tomatoes and water. Bring to a simmer and cover. Lower the heat and simmer for about 25 minutes, or the bulgur is tender, stirring occasionally.

3. Stir in the beans, feta, spinach, and oregano, and cook until the feta is almost melted and the beans warm through. Garnish with feta and oregano to serve.

NUTRITIONAL VALUE PER SERVING

- CALORIES: 617
- PROTEIN: 10.9GRAMS
- FIBER: 12GRAMS
- NET CARBOHYDRATES:6.5GRAMS
- SUGAR ALCOHOL: 14.7GRAMS
- FAT: 55.8GRAMS
- SODIUM: 5 MG
- CARBOHYDRATES: 32.4GRAMS
- SUGAR: 2.7GRAMS

Lunch recipe

14.　Peppery Pork Stew

(Hands-On Time: 10 mins | Cook Time: 5 mins | Servings 6)

Things We Need

- 6-7 lb. bone-in pork shoulder
- 20 garlic cloves, halved
- ¼ cup whole black peppercorns
- Two bottles of red wine (Chianti)
- Six sprigs of Coarse rosemary salt
- 3 tbsps. extra-virgin olive oil

How to Start

1. Use a mortar and pestle to coarsely grind the peppercorns. Use a sharp paring knife to make about 15-20 slits about ½ inch deep and ½ inch wide over the pork surface.

2. Insert garlic halve into each slit and smother the pork with the crushed peppercorns. Place the pork shoulder into a bowl, then add remaining garlic, red wine, and rosemary, cover, and refrigerate overnight.

3. Preheat the oven to 300°F. Remove the pork shoulder from the marinade. Reserve the marinade for later. Pat the pork dry with the help of paper towels and season with salt.

4. Add oil to a Dutch oven and place over medium heat until the oil is hot but not smoking. Brown the pork, fat side down until golden, then flip, add the reserved marinade, and bring to a gentle simmer.

5. Keep into the preheated oven and cook for about 5 hours or until the meat falls off the bone. Pull the meat apart from the oven.

6. Take off the fat from the sauce and season well. Serve with the pork and crusty bread.

NUTRITIONAL VALUE PER SERVING

- CALORIES: 617
- PROTEIN: 10.9GRAMS
- FIBER: 12GRAMS
- NET CARBOHYDRATES:6.5GRAMS
- SUGAR ALCOHOL: 14.7GRAMS
- FAT: 55.8GRAMS
- SODIUM: 5 MG
- CARBOHYDRATES: 32.4GRAMS
- SUGAR: 2.7GRAMS

15.   Fish Chowder

(Hands-On Time: 10 mins | Cook Time: 5 mins | Servings 6)

Things We Need

- 1 lb. skinless tilapia fillets, cut into 2-inch chunks four slices bacon, cut crosswise into
- ½ inch pieces
- 28 oz. plum tomatoes in juice one onion, finely chopped two medium carrots, halved lengthwise and thinly sliced crosswise two medium baking potatoes, peeled and cut into
- inch chunks
- 2 x 8 oz. clam juice
- ½ tsp. dried thyme
- Coarse salt and ground pepper

How to start

1. Using a 5-quart Dutch oven, cook the bacon on medium-low heat for about 10 minutes. Discard all but 1 tbsp. fat; add in the onion and carrots, and cook, occasionally stirring, for about 10 minutes.

2. Crush the tomatoes using the back of a spoon and add to the pot with the juice, clam juice, and 1½ mug water. Bring to a boil.

3. Add the potatoes and thyme reduce the heat and allow simmering. Cook for about 15-20 minutes unless potatoes are tender.

4. Add the fish, and cover it. Cook for about 3 minutes or until flaky—season with salt and pepper.

5. To serve, ladle the stew into six bowls and serve hot.

NUTRITIONAL VALUE PER SERVING

- CALORIES: 617
- PROTEIN: 10.9GRAMS
- FIBER: 12GRAMS
- NET CARBOHYDRATES:6.5GRAMS
- SUGAR ALCOHOL: 14.7GRAMS
- FAT: 55.8GRAMS
- SODIUM: 5 MG
- CARBOHYDRATES: 32.4GRAMS
- SUGAR: 2.7GRAMS

16. Golden Lentil Stew

(Hands-On Time: 10 mins | Cook Time: 5 mins | Servings 6)

Things We Need

- ½ cup dried chickpeas, soaked in water overnight 1 cup yellow lentils, rinsed
- One medium onion, finely chopped four celery stalks, finely chopped four ripe tomatoes, peeled and chopped three garlic cloves, minced
- 1 tbsp. tomato paste
- 2 tbsps. finely chopped cilantro, plus 1 tbsp. coarsely chopped 5 oz. orzo or vermicelli, broken into pieces eight mugs homemade or low-sodium vegetable stock 2 tbsps. extra-virgin olive oil 1 tbsp. lemon juice four mugs water
- ½ cup pitted dates

- One cinnamon stick
- 3 tsps. coarse salt
- ½ tsp. ground ginger
- ½ tsp. sweet paprika
- ½ tsp. turmeric
- ½ tsp. ground coriander ¼ tsp. ground nutmeg
- ¼ tsp. pepper ⅛tsp. ground cloves
- 2 tbsp. coarsely chopped flat-leaf parsley, plus whole leaves for garnish one lemon, cut into wedges

How to Start

1. Use a Dutch oven to heat the oil over medium heat, add onion and cook for 5 minutes. Add in the chickpeas, water, and stock and simmer for 45 minutes or until tender. Combine the garlic, finely chopped cilantro, and salt and mash into a paste. Add the pasta, tomatoes, celery, lentils, tomato paste, lemon juice, and

2. Spices to the oven and simmer for 30-40 minutes. Add the pasta and dates and allow cooking, occasionally stirring until the pasta is al dente. Stir in the coarsely chopped cilantro and parsley. Garnish with parsley and serve with lemon wedges.

NUTRITIONAL VALUE PER SERVING

- CALORIES: 617
- PROTEIN: 10.9GRAMS
- FIBER: 12GRAMS
- NET CARBOHYDRATES:6.5GRAMS
- SUGAR ALCOHOL: 14.7GRAMS
- FAT: 55.8GRAMS
- SODIUM: 5 MG
- CARBOHYDRATES: 32.4GRAMS
- SUGAR: 2.7GRAMS

17. Dutch Oven Pilaf

(Hands-On Time: 10 mins| Cook Time: 5 mins | Servings 6)

Things We Need

- 4 oz. salt pork, slab bacon, or Italian pancetta, cut into ¼ inch thick and diced 3½ lb. chicken pieces
- Two mugs of long-grain white rice, one onion, chopped
- One garlic clove, minced two celery stalks, chopped one whole hot pepper
- Two mugs seeded and diced tomatoes with the juices four mugs low-sodium chicken broth or water ½ tsp. salt
- Two bay leaves
- ¼ tsp. coarsely ground black pepper 1 tsp. each dried thyme, parsley, sage, marjoram 1 tbsp. chopped parsley Rind of 1 lemon

How to Start

1. Rinse the pork well, pat dry and place into a Dutch oven and saut   over medium heat until the pork is browned. Remove all but 2 tbsps. of fat and reserve.

2. Add celery and onion and saut   for about 5 minutes; add in the garlic and saut   for another 30 seconds. Add the broth and increase the heat to medium-high. Bring to a boil, skim off any scum and reduce heat to medium.

3. Add in the chicken, herbs, bay leaves, hot pepper, tomatoes, and lemon zest to the liquid. Allow simmering, covered, for 30 minutes. Remove skin and bone chicken, cut or shred the meat into bite-sized pieces. Reserve 2 tbsps. of fat and discard the balance. Return the chicken to the pot.

4. Wash the rice and drain well. Add to the pot, increase heat and bring the oven to a gentle simmer, reduce heat to low, cover and allow cooking for 30 minutes. Remove bay leaves, hot pepper, and zest, fluff up the rice with a fork. Transfer to a platter and serve immediately.

NUTRITIONAL VALUE PER SERVING

- CALORIES: 617
- PROTEIN: 10.9GRAMS
- FIBER: 12GRAMS
- NET CARBOHYDRATES:6.5GRAMS
- SUGAR ALCOHOL: 14.7GRAMS
- FAT: 55.8GRAMS
- SODIUM: 5 MG
- CARBOHYDRATES: 32.4GRAMS
- SUGAR: 2.7GRAMS

18.　　Pho in a Dutch Oven

(Hands-On Time: 10 mins| Cook Time: 5 mins | Servings 6)

Things We Need

- 1¼ lb. Hickory smoke or honey mustard marinated pork tenderloin 3 oz. country ham or bacon
- Three mugs spinach leaves 6 tbsps. chopped green onions 1 cup shelled Edamame.
- One sweet potato peeled and cubed two onions, slivered
- 2 tbsps. Country mustard 3 tbsps. maple syrup
- Four mugs reduced-sodium chicken broth ½ lb. whole-wheat spaghetti, cooked ½ cup finely shredded Cheddar cheese

How to Start

1. In a Dutch oven, over medium-high heat, cook the country ham for 5 minutes. Remove, then add pork, maple syrup, and mustard and cook for 20 minutes. Remove pork, chop or shred into bite-size pieces.

2. Add the onion to the Dutch oven and saut for 5 minutes; add in the pork, Edamame, sweet potato, and broth. Bring to a boil, then reduce heat and allow simmering for 15 minutes. Stir in the ham and spinach and cook for a minute.

3. Place the pasta into six bowls, top with pork mixture, cheese, and green onions.

NUTRITIONAL VALUE PER SERVING

- CALORIES: 617
- PROTEIN: 10.9GRAMS
- FIBER: 12GRAMS
- NET CARBOHYDRATES:6.5GRAMS
- SUGAR ALCOHOL: 14.7GRAMS
- FAT: 55.8GRAMS
- SODIUM: 5 MG
- CARBOHYDRATES: 32.4GRAMS
- SUGAR: 2.7GRAMS

19.   Banana Bread

(Hands-On Time: 10 mins| Cook Time: 5 mins | Servings 6)

Things We Need

- 1 cup butter
- 1 cup sugar
- Three eggs
- 1 tsp. vanilla extract three medium bananas
- Two mugs flour
- 1 tsp. baking soda

How to Start

1. Preheat the oven to 350°F. Spray a loaf pan with spray of cooking and set aside.
2. Place the Dutch oven into the preheated oven.
3. Cream the butter and sugar together, add the extract and eggs, and mix well. Mash the bananas and add them to the butter mixture.

4. Sift the flour and baking soda together and fold into the butter mixture. Pour into the prepared loaf tin. Remove the Dutch oven and place two bricks into the oven, and place the loaf tin on the bricks. Cover and place into the preheated oven.

5. Bake for 45 minutes or until a skewer inserted into the middle of the loaf come out clean.

NUTRITIONAL VALUE PER SERVING

- CALORIES: 617
- PROTEIN: 10.9GRAMS
- FIBER: 12GRAMS
- NET CARBOHYDRATES:6.5GRAMS
- SUGAR ALCOHOL: 14.7GRAMS
- FAT: 55.8GRAMS
- SODIUM: 5 MG
- CARBOHYDRATES: 32.4GRAMS
- SUGAR: 2.7GRAMS

20.   Dutch Oven Buttermilk Cornbread

(Hands-On Time: 10 mins| Cook Time: 5 mins | Servings 6)

Things We Need

- 12 oz. can creamed corn
- 1 cup buttermilk
- 2 tbsp. shortening two eggs
- Two mugs cornmeal
- 1½ tsp. baking powder
- ½ tsp. baking soda
- 1 tsp. salt

How to Start

1. Preheat the oven to 400° F. Place a 12-inch Dutch oven in the oven to heat.

2. Sift the dry Things We Need into a bowl and add the creamed corn, buttermilk, and eggs and mix thoroughly.

3. Remove the Dutch oven from the heated oven and melt the shortening, then add the batter into the oven allowing the shortening to spill onto the top of the batter.

4. Cover and place into the preheated oven and cook until the bread browns and firms.

5. Allow cooling for about 10 minutes before slicing. Serve warm.

NUTRITIONAL VALUE PER SERVING

- CALORIES: 617
- PROTEIN: 10.9GRAMS
- FIBER: 12GRAMS
- NET CARBOHYDRATES:6.5GRAMS
- SUGAR ALCOHOL: 14.7GRAMS
- FAT: 55.8GRAMS
- SODIUM: 5 MG
- CARBOHYDRATES: 32.4GRAMS
- SUGAR: 2.7GRAMS

21.   Monkey Bread

(Hands-On Time: 10 mins| Cook Time: 5 mins | Servings 6)

Things We Need

- Four cans refrigerated tube biscuits
- 1 cup butter
- ½ cup brown sugar
- 1 cup sugar
- 4 tsps. ground cinnamon
- ¾ cup raisins

How to Start

1. Coat a 12-inch Dutch oven with oil or butter to prevent the dough from sticking.
2. Mix the sugars and cinnamon in a Ziploc bag. Cut each tube of the biscuit dough into quarters. Drop two pieces of the dough into the sugar and shake to coat the dough thoroughly. Remove the dough

from the bag and make a layer in the bottom of the Dutch oven using about half the dough.

3. Sprinkle a layer of raisins over and then place another layer of dough over the raisins and sprinkle the raisins' balance.

4. Butter melt the completely in a saucepan and add in the sugar mixture and mix to form a thin syrup. Pour over the dough coating as much as possible.

5. Baked in a heated oven at 350°F until cooked through.

NUTRITIONAL VALUE PER SERVING

- CALORIES: 617
- PROTEIN: 10.9GRAMS
- FIBER: 12GRAMS
- NET CARBOHYDRATES:6.5GRAMS
- SUGAR ALCOHOL: 14.7GRAMS
- FAT: 55.8GRAMS
- SODIUM: 5 MG
- CARBOHYDRATES: 32.4GRAMS
- SUGAR: 2.7GRAMS

22.   Jalapeno Cornbread

(Hands-On Time: 10 mins| Cook Time: 5 mins | Servings 6)

Things We Need

- Three mugs of yellow cornmeal
- 1½ mugs flour
- 2¼ tbsps. baking powder
- 3 tbsp. brown sugar five eggs
- ¾ cup butter, melted
- 1½ mugs canned corn, drained
- ¾ cup grated cheddar cheese
- ¾ cup grated onion
- ¾ cup jalapenos, finely chopped
- Two mugs of milk

How to Start

1. Preheat the oven to 400°F. Lightly grease a 12-inch Dutch oven and heat in the oven.

2. In a bowl, combine the eggs, milk, and butter. Sift the dry Things We Need together into a mixing bowl.

3. Add the egg mixture to the dry Things We Need and mix well. Add remaining Things We Need and mix to combine.

4. Pour the mixture into the preheated Dutch oven and bake until a toothpick inserted comes out clean.

5. Remove the Dutch oven from the heat and leave to cool for about 15 minutes before serving.

NUTRITIONAL VALUE PER SERVING

- CALORIES: 617
- PROTEIN: 10.9GRAMS
- FIBER: 12GRAMS
- NET CARBOHYDRATES:6.5GRAMS
- SUGAR ALCOHOL: 14.7GRAMS
- FAT: 55.8GRAMS
- SODIUM: 5 MG
- CARBOHYDRATES: 32.4GRAMS
- SUGAR: 2.7GRAMS

23.   Gingerbread

(Hands-On Time: 10 mins | Cook Time: 5 mins | Servings 6)

Things We Need

- 1½ mugs flour
- 1 cup whole wheat flour
- 2 tsps. baking soda
- 1 tsp. cinnamon
- ¼ tsp. salt
- ¾ cup Turbinado sugar
- ½ cup canola oil
- ¼ cup molasses
- ½ cup buttermilk
- 1 cup boiling water
- Two eggs

- ½ cup ginger root, minced

How To Start

1. Preheat the oven to 350°F. Lightly grease and flour a 12-inch Dutch oven.

2. Dissolve the baking soda in the boiling water. Mix the molasses, eggs, oil, and buttermilk in a mixing bowl. Add the baking soda mixture to the molasses mixture.

3. In a separate bowl, sift together the flours, salt, and cinnamon. Fold the dry Things We Need into the wet mixture. Pour all the mixture into the prepared Dutch oven.

4. Place the range into the preheated oven and allow baking until a toothpick inserted comes out clean.

NUTRITIONAL VALUE PER SERVING

- CALORIES: 617
- PROTEIN: 10.9GRAMS
- FIBER: 12GRAMS
- NET CARBOHYDRATES:6.5GRAMS
- SUGAR ALCOHOL: 14.7GRAMS
- FAT: 55.8GRAMS
- SODIUM: 5 MG
- CARBOHYDRATES: 32.4GRAMS
- SUGAR: 2.7GRAMS

24.   Orange-Tomato Couscous with Chicken

(Hands-On Time: 10 mins| Cook Time: 5 mins | Servings 6)

Things We Need

- Six boneless, skinless chicken thighs, trimmed
- 1 cup whole wheat couscous
- One medium onion, thinly sliced
- 1 x 14 oz. can diced tomatoes with juice
- 1 x 15 oz. can chickpeas, rinsed
- 2 tbsps. extra-virgin olive oil, divided
- 1 cup reduced-sodium chicken broth
- ¼ tsp. pepper
- ¼ tsp. salt
- 1¼ tsps. ground cinnamon, divided
- 1¼ tsps. ground cumin, divided

- 4 tbsp. chopped cilantro, divided one orange, scrubbed, halved, and cut into ¼ inch slices

How to Start

1. Season the chicken thighs with salt, pepper, ¼ tsp. cumin, and ¼ tsp. cinnamon.

2. Place 1 tbsp. oil in a 12-inch Dutch oven over medium heat and ads in the chicken thighs and cook until well browned. Transfer to a plate and set aside.

3. Add the remaining oil and onion to the oven and cook, occasionally stirring, until the onion is softened. Add the remaining cinnamon and cumin and cook, stirring constantly.

4. Add the tomatoes with the juice, chickpeas, broth, 2 tbsps. cilantro, and the orange slices. Bring to a simmer, using a wooden spoon to scrape the browned bits on the bottom and sides of the pan.

5. Cover and cook over medium-low heat until the chicken is cooked through.

6. Transfer to a serving platter and try to keep warm.

7. Bring the liquid in the oven to a boil, add in the couscous and place the thighs on top of the mixture. Remove from the heat, cover, and allow

standing for 5 minutes before serving. Garnish with remaining cilantro and orange slices.

NUTRITIONAL VALUE PER SERVING

- CALORIES: 617
- PROTEIN: 10.9GRAMS
- FIBER: 12GRAMS
- NET CARBOHYDRATES:6.5GRAMS
- SUGAR ALCOHOL: 14.7GRAMS
- FAT: 55.8GRAMS
- SODIUM: 5 MG
- CARBOHYDRATES: 32.4GRAMS
- SUGAR: 2.7GRAMS

25. Root Vegetable Stew with Herbed Dumplings

(Hands-On Time: 10 mins | Cook Time: 5 mins | Servings 6)

Things We Need

- Stew
- 2 lb. root vegetables, peeled, diced (beetroot, carrots, parsnips, celeriac, rutabaga, turnips)
- 3 mugs chopped dark, leafy greens (beet, kale, turnip) 8 oz. Italian sausage links, hot or sweet one onion, diced
- Four cloves garlic, minced
- 1 tbsp. chopped sage or rosemary 4 tsps. extra -virgin olive oil, divided four mugs reduced-sodium chicken broth Dumplings
- 1 /2 cup cake flour

- 1¼ mugs whole-wheat pastry flour 1 tbsp. baking powder ¼ tsp. salt
- 1 tbsp. chopped sage or rosemary one egg, lightly beaten ½ cup low-fat milk

How to Start

1. In a medium skillet over medium heat, heat 2 tsps. Oil and add in the sausage, and cook till browned on all sides. Put all these on a cutting board and allow cooling before cutting into 1-inch pieces.

2. Heat the remaining oil in a Dutch oven over medium heat and cook onion, occasionally stirring, for about4 minutes. Add in the prepared root vegetables and cook for 5 minutes. Add in the garlic and sage or rosemary and cook for about 30 seconds. Add in the broth and simmer it, stirring constantly. In a mixing bowl, whisk the flours, sage or rosemary, salt, and baking powder. Add in the egg and milk and stir to form a batter.

3. Once the stew begins to simmer, add in the greensand the sausage and allow simmering. Drop about 1 tbsp. of dough over the stew. Lower the temperature, cover, and allow cooking undisturbed for about 10 minutes. The

4. Vegetables should be tender, the dumplings puffed and the sausage cooked through.

NUTRITIONAL VALUE PER SERVING

- CALORIES: 617
- PROTEIN: 10.9GRAMS
- FIBER: 12GRAMS
- NET CARBOHYDRATES:6.5GRAMS
- SUGAR ALCOHOL: 14.7GRAMS
- FAT: 55.8GRAMS
- SODIUM: 5 MG
- CARBOHYDRATES: 32.4GRAMS
- SUGAR: 2.7GRAMS

26.   Braised Winter Vegetables Pasta

(Hands-On Time: 10 mins| Cook Time: 5 mins | Servings 6)

Things We Need

- Two mugs bite-size cauliflower florets two mugs bite-sized butternut squash cubes 1 x
- 10 oz. bag frozen lima beans, thawed one onion, diced
- Four cloves garlic, minced
- 8 oz. whole-wheat medium pasta shells 2 tbsps. extra-virgin olive oil 1 cup dry white wine
- Four mugs vegetable broth1 tbsp. finely chopped sage ¼ tsp. salt pepper to taste

How to Start

1. Heat oil in a 12-inch Dutch oven over medium heat and add in the onion, garlic, and sage. Cook for 5 minutes, stirring occasionally.

2. Add the wine and broth to the pan and bring to a boil over medium-high heat. Add in the pasta, cauliflower, squash, salt, and pepper. Cook, occasionally stirring, until the pasta is al dente, about 10 minutes.

Add in the lima beans and cook until the lima beans and pasta are tender, and the liquid is absorbed.

NUTRITIONAL VALUE PER SERVING

- CALORIES: 617
- PROTEIN: 10.9GRAMS
- FIBER: 12GRAMS
- NET CARBOHYDRATES:6.5GRAMS
- SUGAR ALCOHOL: 14.7GRAMS
- FAT: 55.8GRAMS
- SODIUM: 5 MG
- CARBOHYDRATES: 32.4GRAMS
- SUGAR: 2.7GRAMS

27. Hard Cider-Braised Lamb Shanks

(Hands-On Time: 10 mins| Cook Time: 5 mins | Servings 6)

Things We Need

- 3 lb. lamb shanks, trimmed
- 3 x 12 oz. bottles hard apple cider 12 whole shallots, peeled, root end trimmed and left intact four cloves garlic, peeled
- Three firm tart apples (Granny Smith, Idared, Cortland), peeled and cut into eight wedges
- ½ cup all-purpose flour
- ¾ tsp. kosher salt
- ½ tsp. pepper one sprig rosemary, plus
- ½ tsp. chopped, divided

- 2 tbsps. extra-virgin olive oil

How to Start

1. Season the lamb shanks with salt and ½ tsp. pepper. Dredge the lamb shanks with the flour in a shallow dish, tapping off any excess.

2. Use a Dutch oven to heat the oil over medium heat. Add in the lamb shanks and cook for 10 minutes, ensuring that all sides are browned. Transfer to a plate and keep aside.

3. Add shallots and garlic to the juices in the pan reduce the heat, cover and allow simmering. Check every 45 minutes to ensure that the shanks are submerged in the liquid. Cook for about 1½ - 2 hours or until the meat is tender.

4. Place the lamb shanks on a serving platter and cover with aluminum foil to keep warm. Allow the sauce to boil on medium-high for 5 minutes, add in the apples, and remaining rosemary. Cook for about 10-15 minutes, stirring occasionally.

5. Return the shanks to the pan and coat with the sauce. Cook until the shanks are heated through. Remove the rosemary sprig.

6. Serve the shanks with boiled rice and the sauce.

NUTRITIONAL VALUE PER SERVING

- CALORIES: 617
- PROTEIN: 10.9GRAMS
- FIBER: 12GRAMS
- NET CARBOHYDRATES:6.5GRAMS
- SUGAR ALCOHOL: 14.7GRAMS
- FAT: 55.8GRAMS
- SODIUM: 5 MG
- CARBOHYDRATES: 32.4GRAMS
- SUGAR: 2.7GRAMS

28. Autumn Chicken Stew

(Hands-On Time: 10 mins| Cook Time: 5 mins | Servings 6)

Things We Need

- 1 lb. chicken tenders, cut into bite-size pieces one onion, chopped
- Two medium carrots, peeled and chopped four medium parsnips, peeled and chopped 2 Granny Smith apples, peeled and chopped four mugs reduced-sodium chicken broth 5 tsps. Extra-virgin oil 2 tsps. cider vinegar ½ tsp. salt
- ¼ tsp. pepper 2 tsps. chopped rosemary

How to Start

1. Place a Dutch oven over medium heat and add the olive oil to heat. Add the chicken, stirring randomly and cook for 5 minutes or until just cooked through. Transfer to a plate and set aside.

2. Add the remaining oil to the pot with the onion, carrots, parsnips, salt and pepper, and rosemary. Cook, occasionally stirring, until the vegetables begin to soften.

3. Add in the broth and apples, and cook for a further 8-10 minutes, stirring often.

4. Add the chicken pieces to the pot and stir in the vinegar.

5. Serve with crusty bread or boiled rice.

NUTRITIONAL VALUE PER SERVING

- CALORIES: 617
- PROTEIN: 10.9GRAMS
- FIBER: 12GRAMS
- NET CARBOHYDRATES:6.5GRAMS
- SUGAR ALCOHOL: 14.7GRAMS
- FAT: 55.8GRAMS
- SODIUM: 5 MG
- CARBOHYDRATES: 32.4GRAMS
- SUGAR: 2.7GRAMS

29.   Seeded Multigrain Boule

(Hands-On Time: 10 mins| Cook Time: 5 mins | Servings 6)

Things We Need

- 2½ mugs whole-wheat flour plus
- 3 tbsp., divided two mugs unbleached bread flour, plus extra as needed
- ½ cup uncooked long-grain brown rice (brown basmati)
- 1/3 cup old-fashioned rolled oats
- 2 tbsps. toasted wheat germ
- 3 tbsps. poppy seeds, divided
- 3 tbsps. sesame seeds, divided
- 3 tbsps. golden flaxseeds, divided

- 4 tbsps. roasted pepitas or sunflower seeds, divided
- 3 tbsps. clover honey or other mild honey
- 2½ mugs ice water, plus extra if needed
- 1¼ tsps. instant, quick-rising
- ¼ tsps. salt
- One beaten egg for glazing

How to Start

1. Grin the rice in a coffee mill or blender until it is a coarse powder and place in a mixing bowl. Add 2½ mugs whole-wheat flour, two mugs bread flour, oats, wheat germ, 2 tbsps. Each flaxseed, pepitas or sunflower seeds, poppy seeds, sesame seeds, salt, and yeast.

2. Whisk in 2½ mugs ice water and honey in a medium bowl and mix well to form moist and sticky dough. Lightly coat with oil, cover with plastic wrap and leave to rise at room temperature for 12-18 hours.

3. Grease a 4-6 quart Dutch oven with oil, sprinkle with whole-wheat flour. Stir the dough to deflate and add flour if it is too moist. Place the dough into the prepared pan.

4. Sprinkle the remaining 1 tbsp. whole-wheat flour over the dough, pat, and smooth—Tuck in the sides to form a round ball, dust with flour as required. Brush the loaf with beaten egg and after sprinkle the remaining seeds over the top.

5. Cut a 2½ inch-deep slit into the dough using a serrated knife.

6. Cover the pot and leave to rise in a warm room until the dough has doubled about 1¼ - 2 hours. Before baking, heat the oven at the temperature of 475°F and position the rack in the oven to the lower third of the oven, about 20 minutes before baking. Reduce the heat to 450°F, sprinkle the loaf with water, and place covered into the Dutch oven into a heated oven. Bake until lightly browned on top, about 56-60 minutes, uncover and bake until a toothpick inserted comes out clean.

7. Cool in the pot on a wire rack for 10-15 minutes; turn out on the rack, and leave to cool. Slice when still warm.

8. Makes one loaf

NUTRITIONAL VALUE PER SERVING

- CALORIES: 617
- PROTEIN: 10.9GRAMS
- FIBER: 12GRAMS
- NET CARBOHYDRATES:6.5GRAMS
- SUGAR ALCOHOL: 14.7GRAMS
- FAT: 55.8GRAMS
- SODIUM: 5 MG
- CARBOHYDRATES: 32.4GRAMS
- SUGAR: 2.7GRAMS

30.   Braised Beef and Mushrooms

(Hands-On Time: 10 mins| Cook Time: 5 mins | Servings 6)

Things We Need

- 4 lb. beef chuck, trimmed it
- Beef chuck cut into 1½ inch pieces
- 2 lb. Cremini mushrooms, cut into ½ inch pieces
- 8 Shiitake mushroom caps, cut into 1/2inch pieces four mugs finely diced onions
- Two cloves garlic, crushed and peeled
- 2 tbsps. tomato paste
- 2 tbsp. sweet paprika
- 2 tsp. chopped marjoram
- 1 cup reduced-sodium beef broth
- 2 tbsps. canola oil

- 1 tbsp. butter
- 1 tsp. salt, divided
- Pepper, to taste 2-3 tsps. finely minced tarragon or dill for garnish

How to Start

1. Preheat oven to 350°F.

2. Add the butter and oil to a Dutch oven and heat over medium heat; add in the onion and garlic and cook, stirring, until the onions are just beginning to brown. Stir in the tomato paste, paprika, and marjoram.

3. Season the beef with plenty of pepper and ½ tsp. salt and add to the Cremini mushrooms' onions.

4. Stir gently and add in the broth, cover, and place into the preheated oven. Bake for 1¾-2½ hours or until the beef is tender.

5. Stir in the Shiitake mushrooms and bake covered for a further 15 minutes. Remove from the oven, uncover and allow standing for 15 minutes.

6. Skim any fat and transfer the beef and mushrooms to a bowl using a slotted spoon. Put the pot back on the stovetop. Bring to a gentle simmer and cook until the sauce coast the back of a spoon. Stir the beef, mushrooms, and remaining

salt to the sauce and heat through. Garnish with tarragon or dill and serve.

NUTRITIONAL VALUE PER SERVING

- CALORIES: 617
- PROTEIN: 10.9GRAMS
- FIBER: 12GRAMS
- NET CARBOHYDRATES:6.5GRAMS
- SUGAR ALCOHOL: 14.7GRAMS
- FAT: 55.8GRAMS
- SODIUM: 5 MG
- CARBOHYDRATES: 32.4GRAMS
- SUGAR: 2.7GRAMS

31. Asopao de Pollo

(Hands-On Time: 10 mins | Cook Time: 5 mins | Servings 6)

Things We Need

- 2¼ lb. boneless, skinless chicken thighs, trimmed and cut into 2-inch pieces
- 2½ mugs brown rice
- One onion, chopped
- One tomato, chopped
- 1 x 8 oz. can tomato sauce
- 1 x 4 oz. jar pimientos rinsed eight pimiento-stuffed green olives, sliced 2 tbsp. capers, rinsed 4 Anaheim or Pablo chili peppers, chopped
- 1 tbsp. extra-virgin olive oil, 1 tsp. sweet paprika 1 tsp. salt
- 1 tbsp. dried oregano eight mugs water

- 2/3 cup packed chopped cilantro

How to Start

1. Heat oil in a Dutch oven over medium-high heat and add chickens, onion, chilies, oregano, paprika, and salt. Cook, stirring until the onions have softened.

2. Add the tomato sauce, tomato, pimientos, olives, capers, and water.

3. Bring the pot to a boil and stir in the rice, reduce the heat to a simmer, and cook uncovered for 35-45 minutes.

4. Stir in the cilantro and serve.

NUTRITIONAL VALUE PER SERVING

- CALORIES: 617
- PROTEIN: 10.9GRAMS
- FIBER: 12GRAMS
- NET CARBOHYDRATES:6.5GRAMS
- SUGAR ALCOHOL: 14.7GRAMS
- FAT: 55.8GRAMS
- SODIUM: 5 MG
- CARBOHYDRATES: 32.4GRAMS
- SUGAR: 2.7GRAMS

Dinner recipes

32.   Braised Lamb Shanks and Eggplant

(Hands-On Time: 10 mins| Cook Time: 5 mins | Servings 6)

Things We Need

- 3 lb. lamb shanks, trimmed
- 1½ lb. eggplant, peeled
- One onion, diced

- One green bell pepper, diced five cloves garlic, minced, divided five plum tomatoes, diced
- 2 tbsp. ground sumac, divided
- 1¼ tsp. salt
- ½ tsp. pepper 2 tbsps. extra-virgin olive oil, divided
- 1 cup water
- ½ cup finely chopped parsley, divided

How to Start

1. Rub the lamb shanks with 1 tbsp. sumac, salt, and pepper. Slice the eggplant lengthwise into ½ inch-wide slices and then crosswise into the one-inch-wide piece. Set aside.
2. Place a 5-6 quart Dutch oven over medium heat and add 1 tbsp. oil to heat.
3. Add the lamb and brown on all sides, turning often.
4. Add the remaining oil to the pan with the bell pepper, onion, two minced garlic cloves, and the 1 tbsp. sumac. Cook until the vegetables soften, stirring often. Return the lamb shanks to the pot with the eggplant, tomatoes, and water.
5. Bring to a boil, then reduce heat to bring to a simmer, cover, and cook, stirring occasionally and

turning the shanks over once. Cook until the lamb for 2 hours or until tender.

6. Remove the lamb to a plate and cover with aluminum foil to keep warm. Increase the heat to medium-high and cook the sauce until reduced and thickened. Remove from heat and add in ¼ cup parsley.

7. In a bowl, mix together the remaining garlic and parsley. Serve over the lamb and vegetables.

8. Serve over mashed root vegetables, brown rice, or bulgur.

NUTRITIONAL VALUE PER SERVING

- CALORIES: 617
- PROTEIN: 10.9GRAMS
- FIBER: 12GRAMS
- NET CARBOHYDRATES:6.5GRAMS
- SUGAR ALCOHOL: 14.7GRAMS
- FAT: 55.8GRAMS
- SODIUM: 5 MG
- CARBOHYDRATES: 32.4GRAMS
- SUGAR: 2.7GRAMS

33. Vinegar-Braised Chicken and Onions

(Hands-On Time: 10 mins | Cook Time: 5 mins | Servings 6)

Things We Need

- 5 lb. skin-on-bone-in chicken (breasts, thighs, and/or legs, breasts halved crosswise) 8 oz. pancetta, cut into ¼ inch pieces 2 lb. Cipollini or pearl onions four garlic cloves, peeled, crushed two bay leaves
- 3 tbsps. olive oil
- ¾ cup balsamic vinegar
- ¾ cup red wine vinegar
- Two mugs low-sodium chicken broth ½ cup golden raisins

- Kosher salt
- black pepper

How to Start

1. In a pot of salted water, cook the onions for 5-10 minutes or until tender.
2. Drain and set aside to cool. Trim ends and peel.
3. Heat the oil in a Dutch oven over medium heat, add in the pancetta and cook until the fat is rendered and the bacon browned. Use a slotted spoon and transfer to a bowl.
4. Add the onions to the pot and cook until just beginning to brown, stirring occasionally. Add garlic and cook, often stirring, for about 3 minutes. Transfer the mixture to the bowl of pancetta.
5. Season the chicken pieces with salt and pepper and brown in batches, 10-15 minutes per batch. Remove and add to the bacon. Drain the fat from the pan and return to the stovetop on medium-high. Add the vinegar to the pan and bring to a boil; add in the broth, raisins, bay leaves, cooked chicken, pancetta, onions, and garlic. Bring to a

boil, then reduce heat and allow to simmer, partially covered for 35-40 minutes, or the chicken is cooked through. Use a slotted spoon and remove the chicken and onions to a platter. Skim the fat from the liquid, remove the bay leaves, and season with salt and pepper. Spoon the sauce

6. Over the chicken and onions to serve.

NUTRITIONAL VALUE PER SERVING

- CALORIES: 617
- PROTEIN: 10.9GRAMS
- FIBER: 12GRAMS
- NET CARBOHYDRATES:6.5GRAMS
- SUGAR ALCOHOL: 14.7GRAMS
- FAT: 55.8GRAMS
- SODIUM: 5 MG
- CARBOHYDRATES: 32.4GRAMS
- SUGAR: 2.7GRAMS

34.   Braised Lamb Shanks with Fennel and Baby Potatoes

(Hands-On Time: 10 mins| Cook Time: 5 mins | Servings 6)

Things We Need

- Six lamb shanks
- Two fennel bulbs (1½ lb.), cut into 1-inch wedges 1 lb. red-skinned potatoes, halved ½ lb. medium carrots, peeled and cut into 3-inch lengths, halved lengthwise if ¼ cup halved green olives, divided four garlic cloves, chopped
- Two anchovy fillets packed in oil, drained, chopped 1 tbsp. tomato paste

- 4 tbsps. olive oil, divided two mugs low-sodium chicken broth 1½ mugs dry white wine or dry vermouth two bay leaves
- ½ tsp. fennel seeds
- 1 tbsp. chopped thyme ¼ cup chopped flat-leaf parsley Kosher salt and black pepper

How to Start

1. Preheat the oven to 325°F and place a rack in the lower third rung of the oven. In a skillet, toast the fennel seeds over medium heat for about 2 minutes. Set aside to cool. Grind in a coffee mill or using a mortar and pestle. Season the lamb shanks with salt and pepper.

2. Use a Dutch oven on medium-high heat to heat the oil. Add the lamb shanks in batches ensuring that they are well browned on all sides. Transfer each batch to a plate as they are done. Reduce the heat to medium-low and add the remaining oil to the pot. Add in the garlic, anchovies, ground fennel seeds, thyme, and tomato paste, and cook for 1 minute.

3. Add in the wine and scrape the pan to incorporate any brown bits from the bottom of the pan. Simmer until the mixture is slightly reduced. Add the bay leaves and broth to the mixture and return the shanks to the pot, "head to toe," to form an even layer.

4. Cover and place the Dutch oven in the preheated oven and braise for 1½ hours. Remove from oven, turn the shanks, add the potatoes, fennel, carrots,

and ¼ cup of olives to the shanks, cover and return to the oven and braise for a further 45 minutes. Transfer the lamb shanks and vegetables with tongs and a slotted spoon to a serving platter. Sprinkle the remaining olives over and cover with aluminum foil to keep warm. Discard bay leaves from the liquid and bring to a simmer, skim any fat and simmer for 15-20 minutes.

5.   Season with salt and pepper and pour over lamb shanks and vegetables. Garnish with parsley.

NUTRITIONAL VALUE PER SERVING
- CALORIES: 617
- PROTEIN: 10.9GRAMS
- FIBER: 12GRAMS
- NET CARBOHYDRATES:6.5GRAMS
- SUGAR ALCOHOL: 14.7GRAMS
- FAT: 55.8GRAMS
- SODIUM: 5 MG
- CARBOHYDRATES: 32.4GRAMS
- SUGAR: 2.7GRAMS

35.Tortilla Soup

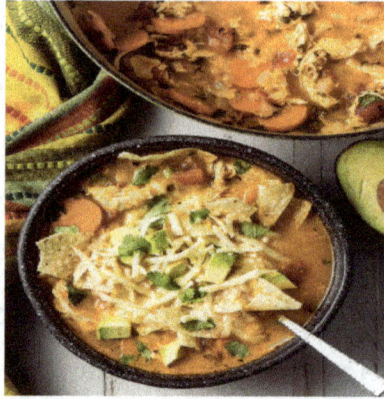

(Hands-On Time: 10 mins | Cook Time: 5 mins | Servings 6)

Things We Need

- 4 lb. chicken
- One carrot, peeled, chopped two mugs frozen corn kernels, thawed one onion, quartered
- Five garlic cloves, minced two dried chipotle chilies
- 1 Jalape o, halved lengthwise seven cilantro sprigs
- 3 tbsp. lime juice five corn tortillas, cut into ½ inch thick strips Kosher salt and black pepper
- Chopped cilantro, halved cherry tomatoes, avocado wedges, queso fresco or mild feta Vegetable oil for frying

How to Start

1. In a Dutch oven, bring the chicken, onion, carrot, garlic, chilies, and 16 mugs of water to a boil. Skim the foam from the surface, reduce the heat and simmer for about 1 hour or until the chicken cooks through. Ensure that the surface is skimmed frequently.

2. Remove the chicken to a plate. Strain the broth, return chilies for a spicier broth and discard the remaining solids. Shred the chicken into a medium bowl and set aside. Discard skin and bones.

3. Replace the Dutch oven on the stovetop with the strained broth on medium heat. Add in the cilantro sprigs and bring the broth to a simmer and cook for about an hour, or the liquid is reduced to about eight mugs.

4. Remove and discard the chilies and cilantro sprigs. Add the lime juice and season with salt and pepper. Add the chicken meat to the broth.

5. Pour oil to about 1 inch into a heavy cast-iron skillet and fry the tortilla chips in batches until crisp and golden. Remove with a slotted spoon and allow draining on paper towels — seasoning

with salt.

6. Cook the corn over high heat on a skillet until some kernels are charred. Heat the broth with the chicken, divide into bowls and top generously with corn, tortilla strips, cilantro, cherry tomatoes, avocado, and crumbled queso fresco.

NUTRITIONAL VALUE PER SERVING

- CALORIES: 617
- PROTEIN: 10.9GRAMS
- FIBER: 12GRAMS
- NET CARBOHYDRATES:6.5GRAMS
- SUGAR ALCOHOL: 14.7GRAMS
- FAT: 55.8GRAMS
- SODIUM: 5 MG
- CARBOHYDRATES: 32.4GRAMS
- SUGAR: 2.7GRAMS

36. Curried Beef Stew

(Hands-On Time: 10 mins | Cook Time: 5 mins | Servings 6)

Things We Need

- Curry Paste
- Six dried Puya or three dried Guajillo chilies, stemmed, seeded one lemongrass stalk, bottom 4 inches only, tough outer layer removed, cut into 1-inch pieces 2 tbsps. Sliced, peeled galangal 2 tbsps. sliced, peeled turmeric
- ¼ cup halved garlic cloves
- ½ cup chopped shallots
- 1 tbsp. Thai shrimp paste ½ tsp. Kosher salt
- Stew
- 2 lb. beef chuck, trimmed and cut into 1½ - 2-inch three cubes of medium carrots, peeled, halved lengthwise, cut crosswise into ¼ inch

thick half-moons 1 cup halved shallots

- 2 tbsp. ground dried Thai chilies six or frozen Kaffir lime leaves 3 tbsp. soy sauce (Thai thin soy sauce) 9 mugs beef broth
- Chopped cilantro
- Thinly sliced Thai basil

How to Start

1. Using a mortar and pestle, pound the chilies and salt together until well combined. Add the lemongrass, galangal, turmeric, garlic, shallots, one after the other, ensuring that each is ground well. Lastly, add the Thai shrimp paste and salt and give the mixture a good pounding.

2. In a bowl, mix together the curry paste, beef pieces, soy sauce, and ground chilies until the beef is well coated.

3. Heat a Dutch oven over medium heat; add the meat to the pan, and cook, stirring, for 5 minutes.

4. Add in the broth and bring to a boil. Turn the heat down to medium, cover, and allow to simmer, occasionally stirring, until the meat is tender but not falling apart.

5. Add in the carrots, shallots, and lime leaves and simmer for about 10 minutes or until the

vegetables are just tender.

6. Garnish with cilantro and basil and serve with boiled white or Basmati rice. S

NUTRITIONAL VALUE PER SERVING

- CALORIES: 617
- PROTEIN: 10.9GRAMS
- FIBER: 12GRAMS
- NET CARBOHYDRATES:6.5GRAMS
- SUGAR ALCOHOL: 14.7GRAMS
- FAT: 55.8GRAMS
- SODIUM: 5 MG
- CARBOHYDRATES: 32.4GRAMS
- SUGAR: 2.7GRAMS

37. Chicken Meatballs with Braised Lemon and Kale

(Hands-On Time: 10 mins | Cook Time: 5 mins | Servings 6)

Things We Need

- 1 lb. ground chicken meat
- Two medium shallots, minced, divided one scallion, minced plus thinly sliced green tops for garnish two cloves garlic, minced.
- One bunch curly kale, remove stems one lemon, very thinly sliced with seed removed
- 2 tbsps. olive oil, divided 1 tsp. salt and black pepper

- ¼ tsp. crushed red pepper flakes two mugs low salt chicken broth.

How to Start

1. Use a Dutch oven to heat 1 tbsp. olive oil over medium heat. Add in the shallots, scallion, garlic, and red pepper flakes and cook for about 6 minutes or until fragrant and soft.

2. Add in 1/3 of the ground chicken meat and cook until through, ensuring that any chunks are broken up. Transfer the meat to a bowl and allow it to cool slightly. Add the remaining chicken meat and season with salt and black pepper. Remove and add chicken to the bowl and mix to combine the meat.

3. Wipe the pot clean using kitchen towels. Add the remaining tbsp. of oil to the pan and heat over medium-high heat until the oil is hot. Form the ground chicken meat into eight meatballs, 2-2½ inch in diameter, and add to the pot. Cook for about 6-8 minutes or until golden on all sides. Remove and place on a plate and set aside.

4. Add the remaining shallot and the lemon slices to the pot and cook until the lemon is tender and begins to turn light golden brown. Add chicken

broth and then the meatballs to the pot.

5. Cover and simmer on low heat until the meatballs are cooked through. Add the kale to the pot and cook until tender but still bright green. Season with salt and pepper. Remove from heat and divide the mixture between 4 bowls topping them

6. With meatballs and lemon slices. Garnish with sliced scallion and serve warm with crusty bread.

NUTRITIONAL VALUE PER SERVING

- CALORIES: 617
- PROTEIN: 10.9GRAMS
- FIBER: 12GRAMS
- NET CARBOHYDRATES:6.5GRAMS
- SUGAR ALCOHOL: 14.7GRAMS
- FAT: 55.8GRAMS
- SODIUM: 5 MG
- CARBOHYDRATES: 32.4GRAMS
- SUGAR: 2.7GRAMS

38. White Bean and Pasta Soup

(Hands-On Time: 10 mins | Cook Time: 5 mins | Servings 6)

Things We Need

- 2-2½ mugs cooked white beans with ¾ cup reserved liquid two mugs chopped onions
- 2/3 cup chopped carrot
- 2/3 cup chopped celery
- One tomato, seeded, finely chopped 1 cup pasta (Farfalle) 3 tbsps. olive oil
- 3½ mugs water
- Extra-virgin olive oil for drizzling

How to Start

1. In a Dutch oven over medium heat, add 3 tbsps. olive oil. Add in the onions, celery, and carrots and saut until the vegetables are soft.

2. Add in 3½ mugs water, beans with the reserved liquid, and tomato. Bring to a simmer, reduce heat to medium-low and allow simmering gently for 25 minutes, stirring occasionally.

3. Add in the pasta and bring to a boil. Cook pasta until al dente, adding more water if required. Season with salt and pepper.

4. Ladle the soup into bowls, garnish with chopped green onions and drizzle with extra-virgin olive oil.

NUTRITIONAL VALUE PER SERVING

- CALORIES: 617
- PROTEIN: 10.9GRAMS
- FIBER: 12GRAMS
- NET CARBOHYDRATES:6.5GRAMS
- SUGAR ALCOHOL: 14.7GRAMS
- FAT: 55.8GRAMS
- SODIUM: 5 MG
- CARBOHYDRATES: 32.4GRAMS
- SUGAR: 2.7GRAMS

39. Soy-Braised Short Ribs with Shiitakes

(Hands-On Time: 10 mins| Cook Time: 5 mins | Servings 6)

Things We Need

- 4 lb. cross-cut beef ribs, about 1 ½ inch thick, cut into two bone pieces ¾ lb. Shiitake mushrooms, stems chopped, caps sliced, divided one bunch scallions, whites chopped, greens sliced, divided 1 x 1-inch piece peeled ginger, thinly sliced ¼ cup brown sugar.
- One cinnamon stick
- Three whole stars anise
- 3 tbsps. vegetable oil, divided 1/3 cup dry sake

- ½ reduced-sodium soy sauce two mugs low-sodium beef or chicken broth Kosher salt and black pepper 8 oz. wide rice noodles, cooked according to package

How to Start

1. Preheat the oven to 325° F and a rack keep in the lower third of the oven. Season the short ribs with salt and pepper. In a Dutch oven on -high heat, add 1 tbsp. oil.

2. Work in batches to cook and brown the ribs, ensuring that the heat is reduced to prevent heat from preventing scorching. Transfer short ribs to a plate.

3. Drain all of the dripping from the pot, reserving 1 tbsp. add the mushrooms, scallion whites, and ginger to the pot, cook, stirring occasionally.

4. Cover and chill remaining mushrooms and scallions. Add two mugs of broth, soy sauce, sake, brown sugar, star anise, and cinnamon, and bring to a simmer. Return the ribs to the pot, bone side up in the liquid in a single layer.

5. Cover and place the pot into the preheated oven. Cook for about 2½ hours or until the meat is fork-tender. Transfer the ribs to a shallow dish, bone

side down.

6. Strain the liquid through a fine-mesh sieve into a measuring jug. Discard the solids and remove any fat from the liquid. Add broth to make 1¼ mug and pour over ribs. Keep it cool, cover with aluminum foil, and chill for at least 3 hours. Preheat the oven to 350° F and bake the ribs, covered, until heated through. Remove ½ cup of the liquid from the baking dish and set aside. Heat the remaining oil in a skillet over medium heat and cook the Shiitake mushroom caps until brown and tender.

7. Add the reserved braining liquid to the pan. Add in the scallion greens, reserving a tbsp., and season with salt. Arrange the cooked noodles on a serving

8. Dish, arrange the short ribs, and drizzle sauce from the plate over. Spoon mushroom with sauce over and sprinkle the remaining scallion greens over.

NUTRITIONAL VALUE PER SERVING

- CALORIES: 617
- PROTEIN: 10.9GRAMS
- FIBER: 12GRAMS
- NET CARBOHYDRATES:6.5GRAMS
- SUGAR ALCOHOL: 14.7GRAMS
- FAT: 55.8GRAMS
- SODIUM: 5 MG
- CARBOHYDRATES: 32.4GRAMS
- SUGAR: 2.7GRAMS

40.   Goulash

(Hands-On Time: 10 mins| Cook Time: 5 mins | Servings 6)

Things We Need

- 2 lb. lean ground beef two mugs elbow macaroni, uncooked two yellow onions, chopped three cloves garlic, chopped 2 x 15 oz. can tomato sauce 2 x 15 oz. can diced tomatoes three bay leaves
- 3 tbsp. soy sauce three mugs water
- 2 tbsp. Italian seasoning
- 1 tbsp seasoned salt
- 1 tbsp. House Seasoning House Seasoning
- 1 cup salt
- ¼ cup pepper

- ¼ cup garlic powder

How to Start

1. Mix all the Things We Need together and store them in an airtight container, and be used to season meat or cook vegetables.

2. Saut the ground beef over medium heat in a Dutch oven until the meat is slightly browned. Break up any chunks and spoon off any fat. Add the onions and garlic paste into the pot and saut for about 5 minutes.

3. Add three mugs of water with the tomato sauce, diced tomatoes, Italian seasoning, bay leaves, soy sauce, house seasoning, and the seasoned salt.

4. Cover the pot and cook it for 15-20 minutes. Add in the macaroni and stir well. Cover and simmer for about 30 minutes. After it, turn off the heat,and remove the bay leaves and leave to sit for 30 minutes before serving with garlic bread and a green salad.

NUTRITIONAL VALUE PER SERVING

- CALORIES: 617
- PROTEIN: 10.9GRAMS
- FIBER: 12GRAMS
- NET CARBOHYDRATES:6.5GRAMS

- SUGAR ALCOHOL: 14.7GRAMS
- FAT: 55.8GRAMS
- SODIUM: 5 MG
- CARBOHYDRATES: 32.4GRAMS
- SUGAR: 2.7GRAMS

41.   Fried Chicken Wings

(Hands-On Time: 10 mins| Cook Time: 5 mins | Servings 6)

Things We Need

- Chicken Appetizer Marinade 5 lb. chicken wings
- Three mugs all-purpose flour
- 5 tsps. salt
- 5 oz. bottle red pepper sauce three mugs buttermilk
- ½ cup plus 1 tbsp. Bayou Blast 2½ tbsps. paprika
- 2 tbsp. salt
- 1 tbsp. black pepper
- 2 tbsp. garlic powder
- 1 tbsp. onion powder
- 1 tbsp. cayenne pepper

- 1 tbsp. dried oregano
- 1 tbsp. dried thyme

How to Start

1. Mix all the Things We Need for the Bayou Blast and store them in an airtight container.
2. Cut the wings at the joints and set the wingtips aside. In a bowl, add all the buttermilk, hot sauce, ¼ cup Bayou Blast, and 3 tsps. salt. Toss the wings in the mixture, coating thoroughly.
3. Cover with plastic wrap and refrigerator for at least an hour or up to 4 hours before proceeding.
4. Preheat the Dutch oven to 360°F with 1-quart peanut oil. To put the flour in a Ziploc bag, add in ¼ cup Bayou Blast and the remaining salt. Place eight pieces of chicken at a time into the seasoned flour and shake to coat well. Remove from the bag and place on a wire rack set over a sheet pan. Continue until all the wings are well coated and leave to sit for 15 minutes.
5. Fry the wings in batches, 10-12 at a time, ensuring that the temperature is increased with the addition of each batch. Fry until the wings are golden brown

6. And cooked through. When all the wings are cooked, sprinkle with the remaining Bayou Blast. Serve hot.

NUTRITIONAL VALUE PER SERVING

- CALORIES: 617
- PROTEIN: 10.9GRAMS
- FIBER: 12GRAMS
- NET CARBOHYDRATES:6.5GRAMS
- SUGAR ALCOHOL: 14.7GRAMS
- FAT: 55.8GRAMS
- SODIUM: 5 MG
- CARBOHYDRATES: 32.4GRAMS
- SUGAR: 2.7GRAMS

Conclusion

The Dutch oven was much loved by the colonials and Native Indians alike for its versatility and durability. It could be used for boiling, roasting, baking, frying, and stews. Recently though the Dutch oven has been replaced with the more advanced kitchen cooking vessels and appliances, however, the great taste of a meal cooked in a thick-walled cast iron pot with a tight-fitting lid cannot be replicated, so the "camp oven" as it is commonly referred to, is still used by many across the globe.

CPSIA information can be obtained
at www.ICGtesting.com
Printed in the USA
LVHW081621090521
686930LV00008B/362